Three

By

Derek Parsons

Cover Art by Lauren Mann

Photograph by Robbi Pfeil

For

Kirsten

Contents

ABILENE 1999

LANDSCAPER

Salty sweat drips
into his mouth,
summer sun bakes skin –

hedge the hollies,
trim the myrtles,
squeeze the hand shears until
sharp throbs stiffen
the bony hand.

Thunk sounds the time clock
like shackles slamming shut
accounting for his minimum wage worth.

Time card placed back on the wall
so tomorrow it can
be eaten away again.

JUDGE PARKS

Judge Parks knew he was dying --
Sitting on his patio
dressed in a white robe and slippers
he watched us plant pansies
in the warm morning sun
through a pair of prescription,
blue-tinted glasses,
his white hair neatly combed,
looking like some kind of philosophical
Marlon Brando as the end
of his cigarette smoldered
to ash.

While we assembled the three-tiered
fountain he had ordered,
he conversed with us about things
which would see irrelevant to a dying man --
football,
how warm October had been so far,
why he enjoyed the sound
of trickling water.

As we left his property
we saw him relaxing,
leaning back into his patio chair
smoking a cigarette
staring into the fountain
watching water drip
then ripple.

HOSPITAL

Fluorescent hum of lights.

I.V. bag.

slow drip.

fluid.

protein

pushed through tiny veins.

23 pound girl.

Narcotics administered.

Pain lessened.

Sleep now possible

while machinery quietly pumps.

Silence slashed

as alarm repeatedly pulses.

I.V. line pinched shut.

Adjustment.

She sleeps.

His thoughts:

Home.

Oatmeal in hair.

Spoiled fits.

Little actions.

Anything.

Hospital hum.

Fluid line drips.

Father watches

the wall clock

timeless.

'88 FORD ESCORT

Lying on my back,
neck burning from holding
my head in awkward positions,
I'm frustrated by this one bolt
on the backside of the starter
which refuses to loosen.

Resting for a moment,
staring up at the tangled
engine block above,
it dawns on me
the bottom radiator hose
must be removed in order
to slide the starter out.

As I wipe caked black gunk
with my index finger from
the right strut, I start thinking
about my life -- how it's just
as knotted as the intertwined
mess of metal and rubber

hanging above, how far

away the silver lining is --

and begin emptying the coolant system.

SIX HOURS*

6:30 a.m.

On the porch
a beetle was dying,
backside to the concrete,
as antennas and legs twitched
in an epileptic display
of natural occurrence.

12:30 p.m.

Limbs kinked inward
to a point, forming
and arthropodic star,
dozens of ants efficiently swarmed,
carrying him in pieces,
single file,
back to their hill.

*Previously appeared in *Rattle, Volume 6, Number 1*

MOTHER'S PRIDE

It's a hell of a thing
waking up before the sun does,
working ten hours,
steam pressing shirts
of businessmen who make
more in one hour than you do
in one day --

Living in your mother's sun-bleached
house at the age of twenty-one,
staring down into coal black pools
that watch you as she suckles
on a bottle,
you wonder if you'll ever
find a way out of the financial muck
to provide for her a life
that doesn't involve jeans
from Goodwill, harassment from those
who can afford better, and an opportunity
to become something better,
because the pain is too much,

your daughter in your place.
You notice your own mother
in the dim kitchen light
making breakfast --
her grey hair and lined face
make sense now,
how she has loved you,
carried unknown burdens for you --
now she watches you
with a mother's pride.

BECOMING

The wind has picked up
today, pushing through
oak leaves like
paper waves crumpling
to shore, and I am reminded
of the day before yesterday
when I picked up my son
from kindergarten.

We walked to the car together,
past a chain link fence,
his small hand in mine,
and said to me
how the wind today
"Sure is strong".

TEMPLE 2008

REBORN

A flash of yellow

      among the brown

striking and bold

      a dandelion in winter.

PEANUT BUTTER

Hundreds,

perhaps thousands,

and hundreds more to come --

peanut butter slides across sliced

bread in pre-dawn light

under a 60-watt bulb

in a kitchen

where countless hours,

and countless more to come,

provide the proving ground

      of parenthood.

SOUNDS

Limbs lie strewn across the yard,
dead and brittle.

Mounds of leaves
lay in un-mowed grass,
browned by winter.

Iron clad clouds cross the sky, featureless,
as squirrels search through old pecans.

The moths have gone,
the cicadas,
the mosquitoes,
crickets,
and I am left
with moaning tires from the highway
       in the distance.

SMELLS

Cigarette smoke,

pungent and raw --

pages of a new book,

bound and held together by glue --

coffee with creamer and sugar --

bitter.

Combined with tobacco --

worse.

Dirt,

mulched leaves,

dusty and sporeous,

the detritus of winter --

but then a breeze

from the north,

where the honeysuckle blooms

along the chain-linked fence --

sweet aroma cuts through it all,

and for a moment

I am delivered.

TESTS

There's this bookcase in the library
that segments the room --
> four foot tall,
> amber stained finish,
> varnish worn from years of use.

I lean on this bookcase
and let it support my weight
as I watch over those
who I've known
for many years, struggle --

years of academic attention for this
one moment,
these two hours,
this one paper --

and when the year's end comes,
they will
leave,
and I will find myself without --

but the bookcase will still stand,

and I will lean on it

hoping the pages

will sustain me.

HOUSTON 2017

TO WRITE A POEM

What a wonderful thing it is
to write a poem
and voyage into the countryside
of language --

how a simple topic,
such as rain,
or a particular encounter,
can be the beginning of a journey
to places unknown --

like how when kids say
"Let's just get in the car and go."
and they do
with no destination in mind.

Where is that willingness now?
Perhaps the world
has become too known --

that to take the winding lanes

of some backwoods highway

off the interstate, where the

trees seem more real because

they are so much nearer the road,

through towns of

unrecognizable names,

where lives are lived

outside the glare of the sun --

Oh to be that kind of king again,

to wield that kind of magic.

SOMEWHERE IN COLORADO

Somewhere in Colorado
there is snow falling
on the limbs
of a Ponderosa
and I wonder if it matters
as I am here
in an entirely different place?

The surrounding forest would
have an eerie quiet
that accompanies snowfall --
the flakes absorbing sound
to where a bird's call
goes no further
than fifty feet --
as if the mass of sound
is suddenly heavier.

I'd like to think the flakes are large --
the type that fall slowly,
like goose down, and rest lightly

on whatever it lands, and that I'd
find a fallen tree
on which to sit
and watch
and be still.

In Houston, it snows maybe once
every five to seven years.
When it does,
if it accumulates, it melts
by noon, but it's a thrill to children,
offering hope of canceled school,
while adults stand in fascination
of a landscape transformed,
like seeing Stonehenge in person --
you wonder if it's somehow
just another picture.

WHO ARE YOU?

There's this poster in my high school
encouraging readers to
"be yourself"
and I wondered exactly
how a 16-year-old
is supposed to know
who they are
when few people
at any age do?

The caterpillar asked this
of me when I was a child,
his fuming hookah
puffing madly,
"Who R U?"
sitting pompous like
on his mushroom,
his insistent manner,
impatient and demanding,
like this poster.
What business of the caterpillar's
was it to ask anyway?

TESUQUE, NEW MEXICO

I am sitting outdoors
north of Santa Fe,
drinking coffee and reading
the poetry of a local resident
as a humming bird,
with feathers that shimmer
like mermaid scales,
samples the flowers
just three feet from me.

I sit motionless.

Life is good.
The morning sun is warm
and the shade is cool
as brilliant white clouds,
who beg for interpretation,
form above the Sangre de Christo Mountains
while I listen to the song
of a bird whose name I do not know.

PICTURES IN A HALLWAY

Walking through the hall
of the administrative office
one can see photos
of students long since graduated.

Here is one of a girl
showing her cow
at a livestock show.

Here is another titled:
Shattered Lives
her face painted white, sitting
cross legged on the ground
holding a large, wooden crucifix,
eyes closed.

These were important moments,
but as some things become,
these photos are invisible
on this wall,
ten years ago now, so says

to the date stamp.

I wonder how significant these

captured moments were?

or did the administration think

they just made for a nice picture?

I wonder if these people, who are now

nearing thirty, living lives

entirely different than

the ones captured here,

know their picture still hangs

in a hallway, and is passed by

hundreds of times a day?

REMOVING CREPE MYRTLE BARK

As you begin to peel
what you'll find beneath
the buckling bark

of a crepe myrtle trunk
is a wood so soft
it beckons you to touch,

to run your thumb and finger
across the soft, pulpy wood,
so fresh in contrast to

the just removed grey,
craggy carapace.
The sensation is so satisfying

you reach again
to liberate the growth
and notice underneath

the mesmerizing pattern of
wood grain running
like rivulets of water

down a window during a rain.
The action becomes obsession
and you peel more

while piles of discarded
bark gather around your feet.
Soon nothing of the old remains.

You've picked it all
like a thick scab you scratch
despite knowing it will only bleed

and reform, but wait just a week
and let the tree take its course
and soon you will have bark to peel again.

SOMEWHERE TONIGHT, JAZZ IS BEING PLAYED

Somewhere tonight, jazz is being played

in a low lit club

full of well dressed

patrons drinking highballs

and old-fashioneds --

> the kind with a maraschino cherry

> instead of syrup

> which is a telling sign

> the bartender isn't lazy.

There would be a crowd

of people squeezing past each other

in the type of frenetic activity

that takes place before

a band is about to play,

> but we would have staked our claim early --

> a table in clear sight of the stage,

> where a bassist waits wearing sunglasses

> as bassists generally do.

A dark-haired waitress
would ask if that would be all?
"Whatever the lady wants."
I'd reply, coolly, nodding to
my wife, whose shoulders my arm
fits comfortably around.

I'd wear a slightly rumpled
corduroy jacket
rather than a slick
black blazer, so people might wonder
exactly what my thing is,

  and as long as I'm fantasizing,

  I'd have a cigarette too, smoothly

  inhaling warm smoke

  followed by a swig of bourbon,
both which burn
in their own way.

PAPAVER RHOEAS

When you came back to bed
I was nearly asleep,
yet noticed something
wasn't right.

You said our cat destroyed
the poppy sprouts, just a few days old.

You collected these seeds
while we were in Italy,
on a walking path between
two villages in the Cinque Terre,
the Tyrrhenian sea flashing
topaz blue,
warm sun,
cool breeze,
terraced vineyards draping
the hillside.

I thought,
as you quietly cried,

this is one of the most

distilled reasons

of why I love you;

this beauty glimpsed

though the eye of a teardrop.

TO PICK DANDELIONS

When I was little
I would pick dandelions,
thinking them beautiful,
from fields or yards
and bring them to my mother
in handfulls,
the wonderment of spring.

When I was older
my children would pick dandelions,
thinking them beautiful,
from the rocky ground outside the apartment,
and bring them to me
in handfulls,
the innocence of childhood.

Now I sit in my yard
and can find no dandelions.
I've killed them all.

And though there are beautiful
irises, poppies, and plumbago,

I do sometimes wish to see,

in the lush conformity

of my suburban lawn,

the simplicity of a brilliant dandelion

and have cause to pick it.

SCIENCE AND GOD

This morning I watched steam
rise from a glass smooth body
of water. At the age of 43,
I can't tell you how that happens --

something about molecules
and temperatures reacting
with one another, phases
of H_2O and such.

I learned about it a million
years ago in elementary school.

Though I can't address the how,
I might could propose why,
but if I did so, I'd risk
giving away too much
and take from you
this wild encounter steeped
deep in the moment, like
summer toes wiggling in
warm river water.

LINES COMPOSED A FEW MILES NORTH OF SANTA FE

There is a cool,

late afternoon breeze

accompanied by the scent

of juniper

as I sit on a patio

over which a pinion

partially hangs.

There is a bumble bee

hovering about the Mexican Sage

and the occasional bird

hops from limb to limb

in a nearby bush.

This all sits very well with me,

goes down like a glass

of sweet summer wine,

the kind so refreshing

a second glass

is never in question.

DOBBIN-HUFSMITH ROAD

Driving to work in the dark
on this two lane, rural road,
occasionally I am witness to
the phenomenon of a brilliant
orange splash whimsically
swirling across the pavement
in the windy wake of the vehicle
in front of me,
and am reminded
that there are still people
who throw lit cigarettes
from cars.

THE LIGHT IS QUIET

The light is quiet this morning,
an attribute not commonly
associated with light, but it is,
nonetheless, that way right now.

In other parts of the house
it comes through in brilliant
shafts, through the cut
glass of the front room windows,
the beginning of the day,
trumpeting loudly
that blessed lesson
of emerging from darkness.

But here, in my reading room,
off to the side of the house,
the light is different,
more understanding,
more gentle,
suitable for reflection.

The brilliance will soon arrive
though, with the frenetic
exuberance that accompanies
such powerful light,
but not yet,
not yet.

SUPER MOON

The first time I heard the term
"Super Moon" was in Florence
the night we dined at Buca Mario.

Walking back to our hotel,
street light reflecting
on the Arno,
we stopped to hear
a U2 cover band play
on the Ponte Vecchio
surrounded by golden
jewelry shops and tiled roofs.

Behind us, following along,
was this moon, in all its
flash bulb brightness. We would stop
occasionally, turn around
and look at it centered over
a bridge with silhouetted cedars
and villas on the hillsides.

I took a few pictures to memorialize
the occasion, thinking it so fantastic
that we saw this Super Moon
while in Florence.

Now I wonder, thinking back,
why it was so special?
I don't know.
It seems any more every full moon
has a special name --
Super, Pink, Blood, Blue, Hunter, Harvest --
as if we have to name
all the things.

What I do know is that
of all the Super Moons
this is the one I remember.

GOOD ENOUGH

I wanted to find words

worthy of being written

on a page, but couldn't,

so I went outside and stood

in the flower bed, moving

the water hose from one hibiscus

to the next. Moments passed

unaccounted before realizing

I was standing

ankle deep in sweet

potato vine, staring at

the Houston moon,

half-full in the sky,

and thought maybe

these words were good enough.

SITTING OUTSIDE AN ART GALLERY IN MADRID, NEW MEXICO

On a red stained deck
sits a potted lemon tree
underneath the shade of an ash
whose leaves cast shadows
that move about the ground
offering evidence
of the cool morning breeze.

Behind me is a small
waterfall that runs into
a glittering pool --
the koi swim about
unaware of the greenery
that reflects above.

There is a plant
growing out of the gutter
that hangs off the maroon
painted trim.
Bushels of dried chili peppers
hang near the door.

Every now and then,

a car passes by,

20 miles per hour.

WELCH'S GRAPE JUICE

1

Each morning I ritually pour
myself a glass of grape juice
to accompany breakfast,
and often think back
to the church of my childhood
which used for communion
grape juice rather than wine,
and so each morning
it's as if I am receiving
the Eucharist in the quiet
light of my kitchen
with a plate of eggs and hash browns.

2

I recall once, when I was a kid,
helping my mom fill the small
communion cups for Sunday's service,
and being stunned to find inside
the church refrigerator

bottles of Welch's grape juice
just like we had at home.
This confused me tremendously,
that something like the blood of Christ
could be bought at the grocery store.

3

When I was young,
My little brother and I simulated
institutions through playing with our
stuffed animals. Sometimes it was school,
where I was the master teacher,
but often times it was church.
One day it occurred to me,
knowing that the Fruit of the Vine
was Welch's, we could serve
it to our plush parishioners.
But alas, mom was worried we would
spill and stain the carpet
a deep purple, impossible to remove.
I should have argued
the blood of Christ covers all sins.

ANOTHER SUNDAY AFTERNOON

It is another Sunday afternoon
and my little friend Lambert
is lying on my lap
as I watch this week's soccer match.

He doesn't want much more
than to sit next to me
on the couch, or the bed,
or wherever he can find me,
and often times I don't want
much more than that either
for the company is good.

He is warm
and as it is December
that is a fact especially welcome.
I can feel his heartbeat
on my thigh and I am struck
by how strong it is,
how this rhythmic thump causes me
to consider that it is this tiny organ
which allows us time together.

He will be 14 next month.

I love him.
I hope that is not too sentimental,
but I am grateful for these
kind of days where I can lay my hand
on his small chest, feel it rise and fall,
his body draped over me
in unconscious trust.

SANDIA PEAK

It is good to be here
      among the pines and aspen,
          the trails and rocks,
              the columbine and juniper.

To the east there is lightning
      and rain on the next ridge.
          Here the breeze is cool,
              the sky above endless,

and these New Mexican
      clouds are infinite in their form and variety.
          Yes, it is good to be here
              and visit with these old
      friends,

where the air is full of the sacred
      and one's mind is allowed to be clear,
          but like all visits, it is too short,
              for honestly, is it ever really
      enough?

IN TRANSITION

Texas doesn't do autumn very well,
but as I travel this stretch
of winding state highway,
I've caught its best attempt
of nature in transition.

It has just rained,
and the countryside is in its Sunday best,
where above the sky is a startling blue,
and a golden afternoon sun flickers
through trees, casting opaque shadows
across the road as I drive
past idyllic farmhouses, lofty Loblollies
and enormous Live Oaks
with their muscular,
twisting arms.

We don't get much color
on the trees in Texas,
maybe a little yellow
from the Pecan or Cottonwood.

Leaves mostly progress

from vibrant to sickly green,

then brown, then drop,

but here, in this moment,

following the road now curving right

with brilliant light covering this meadow,

these rolling hills, this pond to my left,

it is plain that Texas

has its own kind of autumn,

which is hard to see outside

of traveling state highways.

Acknowledgements

I would like to thank the following:

Kirsten Mann, the love of my life, who goes along with my crazy schemes, edits my work, and in all ways is the perfect definition of a better half. Aaron Parsons, who quite emphatically told me, while we were at the bottom of the Grand Canyon no less, that "I should let people read my stuff." My parents Carol, Merle, and Ellie; my children Tyler and Caley, and the daughters of my heart Lauren and Leah, who all love and support me.

Lauren Mann (again!) who worked patiently with me on the design of the book cover. Al Haley, Writer in Residence at Abilene Christian University, who painfully mentored me into the modern world of poetry. The members of the brilliantly named "Writers Circle," Emily Kleypas, Matt Martin, and Stephanie Scherer, who provided me validation in a dark time; thank you for listening to my voice. And finally, my former and present students who are a mirror to myself, who inspire me with their wildly rich and beautiful lives, through which, indeed, I am their student.

For more information, visit parsonspoetry.com

www.ingramcontent.com/pod-product-compliance
Lightning Source LLC
Chambersburg PA
CBHW060653030426
42337CB00017B/2599